MW01591923

Jesus,
I trust in you.

_____

_____

_____

_____

_____

USING THIS PRAYER JOURNAL

This prayer journal provides prompts to guide you through the four traditional forms of prayer, using the acronym ACTS: **A**doration, **C**ontrition, **T**hanksgiving, **S**eeking. Each two-page spread begins with a passage from sacred scripture to provide a moment of meditation. The first of the journaling prompts is adoration, since it is the highest of the four forms of prayer. Contrition is next to recall your sins and ask Our Lord for forgiveness. The thanksgiving prompt is the section to meditate on the many blessings that you have received. Finally the seeking prompt should be used to capture supplications and petitions – a space to share all your needs with Our Lord.

The next page offers some examples of each form of prayer to help you get started. Often, we find ourselves gravitating toward only the 'seeking' or petitioning form of prayer. Take a few moments to familiarize yourself with each form, then plan to set aside specific time for prayer. This journal can be used as a quick 5-minute prayer guide with one minute spent on the bible verse and one minute for each prayer form – or use the journal as a weekly devotional with more time spent in each section, paired with a spiritual reading. However you use this journal – we hope it helps to deepen your relationship with God.

Be anxious about nothing. But in all things, with prayer and supplication, with acts of thanksgiving, let your petitions be made known to God.

PHILIPPIANS 4:6

*All scripture quotations are taken from the CPDV, translation from the Latin Vulgate.

Adoration:

- Praise the Lord for His goodness
- Adore the mercy and forgiveness of God
- Reflect on the wisdom of the Lord
- Praise God for His grace and love
- Think of the statements of adoration in the book of Psalms
- Meditate on the sacrifice of Our Lord Jesus Christ on the Cross

Contrition:

- Confess your sins of the day
- Ask our Lord to show you your predominant fault
- Ask for forgiveness for the sins of your past
- Reflect on the times when you failed to live out the virtues
- Confess any vices or attachment to sin
- Complete an examination of conscience
- Ask Our Lord to help you prepare for death and your particular judgement

Thanksgiving:

- Thank Our Lord for the many blessings you have received
- Consider the spiritual and material gifts you have been given
- Thank God for the gift of faith
- Thank Our Lord for the knowledge of His love
- Ask our Lord to help you appreciate His gifts to you

Seeking:

- Ask Our Lord to grant your petitions and supplications
- Share your needs, concerns, and wants with God
- Pray for yourself, your family, your neighbors, the Church, and all the world

Turn again, my soul, to your rest. For the Lord has done good to you. For he has rescued my soul from death, my eyes from tears, my feet from slipping. I will please the Lord in the land of the living.

Psalm 114:7-9

Notes

Date......................

Adoration...

Contrition...

Thanksgiving...

Seeking...

Before I formed
you in the womb,
I knew you...

Jeremiah 1:5

Notes

....

....

....

Date........................

Adoration...

_____

_____

_____

_____

Contrition...

_____

_____

_____

_____

Thanksgiving...

_____

_____

_____

_____

Seeking...

_____

_____

_____

_____

Let everything whatsoever that you do, whether in word or in deed, be done all in the name of the Lord Jesus Christ, giving thanks to God the Father through him.

Colossians 3:17

Notes

....

....

....

Date.....................

Adoration...

_____

_____

_____

_____

Contrition...

_____

_____

_____

_____

Thanksgiving...

_____

_____

_____

_____

Seeking...

_____

_____

_____

_____

Then may the Lord of peace himself give you an everlasting peace, in every place. May the Lord be with all of you.

2 Thess. 3:16

Notes

Date......................

Adoration...

_____

_____

_____

_____

Contrition...

_____

_____

_____

_____

Thanksgiving...

_____

_____

_____

_____

Seeking...

_____

_____

_____

_____

And so shall the peace of God, which exceeds all understanding, guard your hearts and minds in Christ Jesus.
Phil 4:7

Notes

....

....

....

Date........................

Adoration...

_____

_____

_____

_____

Contrition...

_____

_____

_____

_____

Thanksgiving...

_____

_____

_____

_____

Seeking...

_____

_____

_____

_____

Give joy to the soul of your servant, for I have lifted up my soul to you, Lord. For you are sweet and mild, Lord, and plentiful in mercy to all who call upon you.

Psalm 85:4-5

Notes

Date......................

Adoration...

_____

_____

_____

_____

_____

Contrition...

_____

_____

_____

_____

Thanksgiving...

_____

_____

_____

_____

Seeking...

_____

_____

_____

_____

And so may the God of hope fill you with every joy and with peace in believing, so that you may abound in hope and in the virtue of the Holy Spirit.

Romans 15:30

Notes

....

....

....

Date.....................

Adoration...

_____

_____

_____

_____

Contrition...

_____

_____

_____

_____

Thanksgiving...

_____

_____

_____

_____

Seeking...

_____

_____

_____

_____

Into your hands, I commend my spirit. You have redeemed me, O Lord, God of truth.

Psalm 30:6

Date.....................

Adoration...

Contrition...

Thanksgiving...

Seeking...

Whatever is true, whatever is chaste, whatever is just, whatever is holy, whatever is worthy to be loved, whatever is of good repute, if there is any virtue, if there is any praiseworthy discipline: meditate on these.

Phil 4:8

Notes

....

....

....

Date.......................

Adoration...

Contrition...

Thanksgiving...

Seeking...

...O Lord, demonstrate your ways to me, and teach me your paths. Direct me in your truth, and teach me. For you are God, my Savior, and I remain with you all day long.

Psalm 24:4-5

Notes

Date............................

Adoration...

Contrition...

Thanksgiving...

Seeking...

The night has
passed, and the day
draws near.
Therefore, let us cast
aside the works of
darkness, and be
clothed with the
armor of light.

Romans 13:12

Notes

....

....

....

Date........................

Adoration...

_____

_____

_____

_____

Contrition...

_____

_____

_____

_____

Thanksgiving...

_____

_____

_____

_____

Seeking...

_____

_____

_____

_____

The troubles of
my heart have been
multiplied. Deliver me
from my needfulness.
See my lowliness and
my hardship, and
release all my offenses.

Psalm 24:17-18

Notes

....

....

....

Date.....................

Adoration...

_____

_____

_____

_____

Contrition...

_____

_____

_____

_____

Thanksgiving...

_____

_____

_____

_____

Seeking...

_____

_____

_____

_____

Heaven and earth shall pass away. But my words shall not pass away.

Luke 21:33

Notes

Date.......................

Adoration...

_____

_____

_____

_____

_____

Contrition...

_____

_____

_____

_____

_____

Thanksgiving...

_____

_____

_____

_____

_____

Seeking...

_____

_____

_____

_____

_____

Preserve my soul and rescue me. I will not be ashamed, for I have hoped in you.

Psalm 24:20

Date........................

Adoration...

_____

_____

_____

_____

Contrition...

_____

_____

_____

_____

Thanksgiving...

_____

_____

_____

_____

Seeking...

_____

_____

_____

_____

The troubles of
my heart have been
multiplied. Deliver me
from my needfulness.
See my lowliness and
my hardship, and
release all my offenses.

Psalm 24:17-18

Notes

Date......................

Adoration...

_____

_____

_____

_____

Contrition...

_____

_____

_____

Thanksgiving...

_____

_____

_____

Seeking...

_____

_____

_____

For whatever was written, was written to teach us, so that, through patience and the consolation of the Scriptures, we might have hope.

Romans 15:4

Notes

Date.........................

Adoration...

_____

_____

_____

_____

_____

Contrition...

_____

_____

_____

_____

Thanksgiving...

_____

_____

_____

_____

Seeking...

_____

_____

_____

_____

O Lord, reveal to us your mercy, and grant to us your salvation. I will listen to what the Lord God may be saying to me. For he will speak peace to his people...

Psalm 84:8-9

Notes

Date.....................

Adoration...

_____

_____

_____

_____

Contrition...

_____

_____

_____

_____

Thanksgiving...

_____

_____

_____

_____

Seeking...

_____

_____

_____

_____

O Lord, reveal to us your mercy, and grant to us your salvation. I will listen to what the Lord God may be saying to me. For he will speak peace to his people...

Psalm 84:8-9

Date.........................

Adoration...

Contrition...

Thanksgiving...

Seeking...

And the Angel said to her: Do not be afraid, Mary, for you have found grace with God. Behold, you shall conceive in your womb, and you shall bear a son, and you shall call his name JESUS.

Luke 1:30-31

Notes

....

....

....

Date.....................

Adoration...

_____
_____
_____
_____

Contrition...

_____
_____
_____
_____

Thanksgiving...

_____
_____
_____
_____

Seeking...

_____
_____
_____
_____

And behold, your cousin Elizabeth has herself also conceived a son, in her old age. And this is the sixth month for her who is called barren. For no word will be impossible with God.

Luke 1:30-31

Date.....................

Adoration...

_____

_____

_____

_____

Contrition...

_____

_____

_____

_____

Thanksgiving...

_____

_____

_____

_____

Seeking...

_____

_____

_____

_____

Then Mary said: "Behold, I am the handmaid of the Lord. Let it be done to me according to your word." And the Angel departed from her.

Luke 1:38

Notes

....

....

....

Date.....................

Adoration...

_____

_____

_____

_____

Contrition...

_____

_____

_____

_____

Thanksgiving...

_____

_____

_____

_____

Seeking...

_____

_____

_____

_____

Confess to the Lord,
for he is good, for his
mercy is forever.

Psalm 117:29

Date.....................

Adoration...

___

Contrition...

___

Thanksgiving...

___

Seeking...

___

The Lord is near to
all who call upon him,
to all who call upon him
in truth. He will do the
will of those who fear
him, and he will heed
their supplication and
accomplish their
salvation.

Psalm 144:18-19

Notes

....

....

....

Date.....................

Adoration...

Contrition...

Thanksgiving...

Seeking...

...And Elizabeth was filled with the Holy Spirit. And she cried out with a loud voice and said: Blessed are you among women, and blessed is the fruit of your womb.

Luke 1:41-42

Notes

....

....

....

Date.....................

Adoration...

_____

_____

_____

_____

Contrition...

_____

_____

_____

_____

Thanksgiving...

_____

_____

_____

_____

Seeking...

_____

_____

_____

_____

The Lord founded the earth on wisdom. He secured the heavens with prudence.

Proverbs 3:19

Date......................

Adoration...

_____

_____

_____

_____

Contrition...

_____

_____

_____

_____

Thanksgiving...

_____

_____

_____

_____

Seeking...

_____

_____

_____

_____

With my whole heart,
I have sought you. Do
not let me be driven
away from your
commandments. I have
hidden your eloquence
in my heart, so that I
may not sin against
you.

Psalm 118:10-11

Notes

Date.........................

Adoration...

_____

_____

_____

_____

_____

Contrition...

_____

_____

_____

_____

_____

Thanksgiving...

_____

_____

_____

_____

_____

Seeking...

_____

_____

_____

_____

_____

And suddenly there was with the Angel a multitude of the celestial army, praising God and saying, "Glory to God in the highest, and on earth peace to men of good will."

Luke 2:13-14

Notes

....

....

....

Date....................

Adoration...

Contrition...

Thanksgiving...

Seeking...

For unto us a child is born, and unto us a son is given. And leadership is placed upon his shoulder. And his name shall be called: wonderful Counselor, mighty God, father of the future age, Prince of Peace.

Isaiah 9:6

Notes

....

....

....

Date.........................

Adoration...

_____

_____

_____

_____

Contrition...

_____

_____

_____

_____

Thanksgiving...

_____

_____

_____

_____

Seeking...

_____

_____

_____

_____

And the Word became flesh, and he lived among us, and we saw his glory, glory like that of an only-begotten Son from the Father, full of grace and truth.

John 1:14

Notes

Date.....................

Adoration...

_____

_____

_____

_____

Contrition...

_____

_____

_____

_____

Thanksgiving...

_____

_____

_____

_____

Seeking...

_____

_____

_____

_____

And behold, there was a voice from heaven, saying: "This is my beloved Son, in whom I am well pleased."

Matthew 3:17

Date.....................

Adoration...

Contrition...

Thanksgiving...

Seeking...

The heavens describe
the glory of God, and the
firmament announces the
work of his hands.

Psalm 18:2

Notes

....

....

....

Date......................

Adoration...

Contrition...

Thanksgiving...

Seeking...

...And he said, "Behold, I see the heavens opened, and the Son of man standing at the right hand of God."

Acts 7:55

Date.......................

Adoration...

_____

_____

_____

_____

Contrition...

_____

_____

_____

Thanksgiving...

_____

_____

_____

Seeking...

_____

_____

_____

...Fear God,
and observe his
commandments.
This is everything
for man.

Ecclesiastes 12:13

Date...................

Adoration...

_____

_____

_____

_____

Contrition...

_____

_____

_____

Thanksgiving...

_____

_____

_____

Seeking...

_____

_____

_____

His mother said to the servants, "Do whatever he tells you."

John 2:5

Notes

Date.........................

Adoration...

Contrition...

Thanksgiving...

Seeking...

Because of this, God has also exalted him and has given him a name which is above every name, so that, at the name of Jesus, every knee would bend...

Phil 2:9-10

Notes

....

....

....

Date.....................

Adoration...

Contrition...

Thanksgiving...

Seeking...

And Jesus, calling to himself a little child, placed him in their midst. And he said: Amen I say to you, unless you change and become like little children, you shall not enter into the kingdom of heaven.

Matt 18:2-3

Notes

....

....

....

Date.......................

Adoration...

_____

_____

_____

_____

_____

Contrition...

_____

_____

_____

_____

Thanksgiving...

_____

_____

_____

_____

Seeking...

_____

_____

_____

_____

O Lord, our Lord,
how admirable is your
name throughout all
the earth.

Psalm 8:10

Notes

Date.........................

Adoration...

_____

_____

_____

_____

_____

Contrition...

_____

_____

_____

_____

Thanksgiving...

_____

_____

_____

_____

Seeking...

_____

_____

_____

_____

And he was transfigured before them. And his face shined brightly like the sun. And his garments were made white like snow.

Matt 17:2

Notes

....

....

....

Date......................

Adoration...

Contrition...

Thanksgiving...

Seeking...

I will confess to you, O Lord my God, with my whole heart. And I will glorify your name in eternity.

Psalm 85:12

Date.........................

Adoration...

_____

_____

_____

_____

Contrition...

_____

_____

_____

_____

Thanksgiving...

_____

_____

_____

_____

Seeking...

_____

_____

_____

_____

And taking bread, he gave thanks and broke it and gave it to them, saying: "This is my body, which is given for you. Do this as a commemoration of me."

Luke 22:19

Notes

....

....

....

Date.....................

Adoration...

Contrition...

Thanksgiving...

Seeking...

And taking the chalice, he gave thanks. And he gave it to them, saying: Drink from this, all of you. For this is my blood of the new covenant, which shall be shed for many as a remission of sins.

Matt 26:27-28

Notes

....

....

....

Date........................

Adoration...

Contrition...

Thanksgiving...

Seeking...

And you, Lord God, are compassionate and merciful, being patient and full of mercy and truthful.

Psalm 85:15

Date.......................

Adoration...

_____

_____

_____

_____

Contrition...

_____

_____

_____

_____

Thanksgiving...

_____

_____

_____

_____

Seeking...

_____

_____

_____

_____

And they went to a country estate, by the name of Gethsemani. And he said to his disciples, "Sit here, while I pray." And he took Peter, and James, and John with him. And he began to be afraid and wearied.

Mark 14:32-33

Notes

....

....

....

Date........................

Adoration...

_____

_____

_____

_____

Contrition...

_____

_____

_____

_____

Thanksgiving...

_____

_____

_____

_____

Seeking...

_____

_____

_____

_____

He humbled himself,
becoming obedient
even unto death, even
the death of the
Cross.

Phil 2:8

Notes

....

....

....

Date.........................

Adoration...

_____

_____

_____

_____

_____

Contrition...

_____

_____

_____

_____

Thanksgiving...

_____

_____

_____

_____

Seeking...

_____

_____

_____

_____

Then the Angel responded by saying to the women: "Do not be afraid. For I know that you are seeking Jesus, who was crucified. He is not here. For he has risen, just as he said. Come and see the place where the Lord was placed.

Matt 28:5-6

Notes

....

....

....

Date.........................

Adoration...

Contrition...

Thanksgiving...

Seeking...

...All the ends of the earth have seen the salvation of our God. Sing joyfully to God, all the earth. Sing and exult, and sing psalms.

Psalm 97:3-4

Notes

....

....

....

Date.....................

Adoration...

_____

_____

_____

_____

_____

Contrition...

_____

_____

_____

_____

Thanksgiving...

_____

_____

_____

_____

Seeking...

_____

_____

_____

_____

Great are the works
of the Lord, exquisite
in all his intentions.

Psalm 110:2

Notes

Date.........................

Adoration...

_____

_____

_____

_____

Contrition...

_____

_____

_____

Thanksgiving...

_____

_____

_____

Seeking...

_____

_____

_____

So may the God of patience and solace grant you to be of one mind toward one another, in accord with Jesus Christ, so that, together with one mouth, you may glorify the God and Father of our Lord Jesus Christ.

Romans 15:5-6

Notes

....

....

....

Date.......................

Adoration...

Contrition...

Thanksgiving...

Seeking...

From the rising of the sun, even to its setting, praiseworthy is the name of the Lord.

Psalm 112:3

Notes

Date.........................

Adoration...

Contrition...

Thanksgiving...

Seeking...

The sorrows of death have surrounded me, and the perils of Hell have found me. I have found tribulation and sorrow. And so, I called upon the name of the Lord. O Lord, free my soul.

Psalm 114:3-4

Notes
....
....
....

Date.........................

Adoration...

Contrition...

Thanksgiving...

Seeking...

And we know the present time, that now is the hour for us to rise up from sleep. For already our salvation is closer than when we first believed.

Romans 13:11

Notes

....

....

....

Date.......................

Adoration...

_____

_____

_____

_____

Contrition...

_____

_____

_____

_____

Thanksgiving...

_____

_____

_____

_____

Seeking...

_____

_____

_____

_____

The night has passed, and the day draws near. Therefore, let us cast aside the works of darkness, and be clothed with the armor of light.

Romans 13:12

Notes

....

....

....

Date...........................

Adoration...

Contrition...

Thanksgiving...

Seeking...

Made in United States
North Haven, CT
05 December 2021

12035395R00059